ACTIVATE

Building a Purposeful & Profitable Brand
in a Tribe-Based Digital Culture

RAINAH DAVIS

Copyright © 2019 by Rainah Davis

All rights reserved. No part of this publication may be reproduced, distributed, or transmitted in any form or by any means, including photocopying, recording, or other electronic or mechanical methods, without the prior written permission of the publisher, except in the case of brief quotations embodied in critical reviews and certain other noncommercial uses permitted by copyright law.

Published by:
G.C. Simmons Publishing
Raleigh, North Carolina

Editors: Dr. Gerald C. Simmons
        Dr. Cherie Graham
        Dr. Erin Almond
Editorial Assistants: G. Caroline Simmons
Layout Designer: Erica Smith
Front Cover Artwork: Brittany Oliver Annis
Back Cover Artwork: Rainah Davis

ISBN: 978-0-9984271-8-8

*Dedicated to all my children—
Chynah, Rubie, Amirah, Adiyah, Braxton,
Jamera, Denzel, Matthew, and Joseph.*

Author's Note

I spent almost two years learning everything I could about branding, digital marketing, social media channels, and tribes. I have read books, followed Influencers on social media, downloaded online courses, read academic articles, attended conferences, and completed countless assignments to complete my graduate studies. I did all of that so now you don't have to!

I will share my sources with you. Please read the books, articles, and materials that you want to know more about but please do not feel as if you have to re-read everything that I have. My goal is to help you get started. I want you to understand branding, tribes, super fans, digital media, and content development. These terms are thrown around a lot today, but it is not often clear exactly what they mean in general, and what they mean for you specifically. I specifically chose to study these terms so I could help all of us create brands that could exist in a digital world.

I am just like many of you. I do not have thousands of social media followers; however, I have built a business that has sustained my family after an unexpected job loss. As a matter of fact, I have been able to replace my old income, spend more time with my family and employ others; which means the world to me.

Lastly, I am always on an insatiable quest for knowledge, strategies, and information. I work extremely hard to stay on top of the ever-changing social trends. At the time of this writing, my teenagers are creating TikTok videos. Haven't heard of it? Me either until days before this book went to print in September 2019. According to Livemint, "TikTok, the app promoted by China's ByteDance, is the Twitter of videos. It is easy to use and the app's features allow anybody to make short videos, the 15-second ones being the most popular format, and post them online or share them through various other apps."

See, there is always something to learn when it comes to digital media. The goal is not necessarily to know everything, but to have a foundational understanding that can help you activate your own brand. Whether you have been laid off, need extra income, or have a business/business idea that you believe can support you better than your current 9-to-5, I am confident that the tools in this book will help you and those connected to you.

Let's go!

Rainah

Quick Note about References that you will see in this book:

If you see an author and a year and you want more information about them, please check the references in the back of the book. Those are most likely the academic journal authors and the years that they were written. The primary book sources are practitioners and I will generally list their name, the book name, and the publishing year in hopes that you will add those to your own library.

Contents

Introduction: My Story 1

Section I: Let's Talk About Branding 7

1: Branding Defined 9

2: Great Brand Characteristics 17

3: Tribes, Super Fans, & Audience = Meaningful Brands ... 27

4: Designing a Dynamic Customer Experience 41

Section II: Activate Your Brand 53

5: Activate Your Brand 55

6: Activating Yourself 63

7: Activate Your Business 101:
Business Set-Up, Idea Implementation, and
Accepting Payments 69

Bonus: Two Essential Lists for
Business Owners and Activate Help 89

Introduction
MY STORY

In October 2016, I was laid off from my job, and for months, I spent hours applying for positions and submitting resumes to no avail. I was unable to land a job, but I was not entirely without work.

Back in 2004, I faced a different challenge, one that that many mothers face today. I had three daughters (at the time), and two of them were in daycare. I felt as though I was working only to pay for childcare services! I needed to do something to earn extra money, but like many working moms, I really could not find a second job that would allow me to still be able to take care of my children. So I came up with an alternative solution: I started bartering my marketing and graphic design skills with other business owners whose services that I could use. So in the beginning, I worked with the two types of businesses that I needed the most: daycare providers and hair stylists. My daughters had a lot of hair, and, I am no beautician. I believe that my oldest daughter is the amazing stylist and "weavologist" (urban word to describe a hair dresser that adds extensions and bundles typically by sewing the in the additional hair) because number one: I was just so bad at doing their hair (so she had plenty of practice), and number two—she is genetically-inclined and comes from generations of hair dressers; but needless to say, I helped her find her gift faster.

Getting back to the story—after I helped those business owners and a few friends with logo projects, and they told their friends; all of a sudden, I was creating logos and business cards almost every week. Some of these logos are in still in use today!

As a result of that period in my life, I became good at helping individuals get their ideas out of their head and bring those concepts to life, and I loved doing it. As my daughters aged out of daycare I started working full-time, and eventually put my business on the back burner. The business, initially called Vision Marketing & Design, was later renamed and rebranded as Raindrop Creative many years later.

Times have changed, and branding and online marketing are both critical components to growing and sustaining a business.

Fast forward, years later, I started working on the business again, this time purely as a side hustle. This time I was not alone, as the company became a family affair. In 2014, we added another component to our marketing and branding business, which was content development. We went from helping clients with editing and blogs into writing book devotionals and entire manuscripts. Keep in mind, I re-started this business while working a full-time job. Raindrop Creative opened sister agency called Start Write Publish (startwriteaway.com), and what started as content and editing service, has quickly developed into it a one-stop-shop for authors to get help with writing, editing, and publishing their printed manuscript or e-book. The company began to generate significant revenue while I was trying to find a traditional job in the fall/winter of 2016. Our family business grew and now has a contracted staff that help produce visions for others through our branding agency, in addition to providing publishing and consultation services. We have taken the time to develop an elite group of individuals who are passionate about helping others turn their side hustles and ideas into sustainable businesses.

The company's profitability increased again the next year when I started pursuing my graduate studies in Communications. The more I learned about digital media, culture, tribes, and branding, the more I wanted to share my coursework and research findings with others. This book is the simplified version of my thesis, carefully selected to be able to present information that will help all of us navigate the changing economic and digital landscapes.

My desire is that through strategic brand development and alignment, I can help every reader activate his or her brand and

ACTIVATE

create a business or side hustle that creates additional income, but that also leaves a lasting impact on communities, families, and generations to come.

OVERVIEW

CHANGING ECONOMIC LANDSCAPE

In today's uncertain economic landscape, more individuals are starting businesses and providing contracted services. The "start-up" and "side-hustle" economy is significant across all racial, gender, and class groups. It is more critical than ever to have communication plans for entrepreneurs so that they can not only create a purposeful brand, but take the necessary steps to achieve profitability as quickly as possible. Just as Costin (2012) points out, "entrepreneurship has a critical role not only for economic development but also for the general progress of the society [and] the general progress of any country."

The intended purpose of this book is to enable entrepreneurs to create effective communication strategies that will provide actionable steps to develop and maintain a brand that offers both impact and income. It is also designed to assist entrepreneurs in leveraging relationships with more established companies and influencers to gain access to new audiences. Finally, through the presentation of research-driven concepts, this book will serve as a resource for start-ups and other businesses which seek an enhanced strategy to create impact and obtain profitability in a strategic, systematic way. The first step in achieving this goal is understanding branding.

SECTION I
LET'S TALK ABOUT BRANDING

CHAPTER 1
BRANDING DEFINED

UNDERSTANDING THE DEFINITION OF BRANDING

The initial, most significant challenge entrepreneurs face is not truly understanding what *branding* is. During my coursework I was introduced to several authors and practitioners that changed my entire understanding of branding and digital marketing. One of those authors is Denise Yohn. She provides a profound, yet simple definition of branding: "simply put, your brand is what your company *does and how you do it*. Your brand is not what you say you are—it's what you do." The ability to develop a profitable and robust brand is not only about advertising and identity marks, such as logos as carefully chosen color palettes.

The items above are commonly mistaken as your brand when in reality those items are a part of the brand identity. Identity marks, logos, and promotional items are still a very critical part of your brand. As a matter of fact, David Airey

(2015) explains that there are seven elements needed to create what he defines as an "iconic brand identity." Those seven components, are what he describes affectionately as "the seven ingredients of your signature dish." Those ingredients are:

- **Keep it simple**
- **Make it relevant**
- **Incorporate tradition**
- **Aim for distinction**
- **Make it memorable**
- **Think small** (it should be able to be minimized without losing detail)
- **Focus on one thing** (one feature is better than two, three or more to make it stand out)

The key is to know the rules first. Pablo Picasso said, "Learn the rules like a pro, so you can break them like an artist." Lastly, Airey does suggest there are cases to break the rules, but those times should be the exception and not the rule.

The main point is that no matter how iconic your brand identity may appear, the brand's success will primarily depend upon the company's ability to provide consistent positive customer experiences. Because a brand is not what you say it is, it is what your audience says that it is. It is how they "feel" about what you are offering and ultimately it is about the trust they give you and the experiences that you give them. Branding is ultimately the great trust/experience exchange.

BRANDING THROUGH EXPERIENCES

In *Brand Like a Rock Star*, Steve Jones explains, "Rock star brands don't sell products or services they sell experiences." Jones illustrates his point by using the brand Harley Davidson as an example: "Harley Davidson doesn't sell motorcycles... [it] sells the opportunity for an accountant to be cool, dress in leather, and be even a little scary."

"Experiences" will be one the most important business factors in the digital age, and Brian Solis describes the impact masterfully in his book *WTF: What's the Future of Business*. Now, in addition to be assigned this book for one of my graduate classes, I also got the opportunity to hear a keynote from him at the same Social Media and Marketing World conference that I heard Pat Flynn give the "Super Fans" presentation (which I share more about in Chapter 2). Solis spoke passionately about the creation of the Internet, including the good, the bad, and the ugly. He explains that society looks at their screens about 1500 times per week and how technology is creating a society of digital introverts. These facts are important because how people communicate with each other, also impacts how they communicate with businesses and brands. In the book, Solis introduced a concept called Generation-C.

BRANDING FOR *EXPERIENCE-DRIVEN* GENERATION-C

Solis starts the Generation-C conversation by explaining to

readers that technology is now an extension of humanity but pivots into introducing a "plot twist" on the melodrama that is constantly be spun regarding the multi-generational chaotic tailspin that companies are in trying to appeal to five generations (traditionalists, baby boomers, Gen X, Gen Y (millennials) and now Gen Z). Solis drops the label Generation C to describe a new group of "connected consumers who have crossed over and embraced the digital lifestyle." Generation C is defined as a connected society who shares similar interests and behavior. Solis explains that Generation C is growing as a market share and rely on the experiences of others in their buying decisions. This group uses reviews to determine purchases, they look up places that their friends "check into" online, they look for coupons online before making a purchase, and they rely on the experiences of "like-minded strangers" to determine their actions and decisions about a brand. This viewpoint is a consumer segment to consider when designing online experiences.

BRANDING FOR THE DIGITAL COMMUNITY

For entrepreneurs to create purposeful and impactful brands that lend to profitability sooner rather than later, it is crucial to understand the importance of marketing communications in today's digital business landscape. Rowley (2004) explains that the digital marketing community needs three aspects for success:

1. Creating a presence (awareness building)
2. Creating relationships (establishing experiences)
3. Creating mutual value (discovering and utilizing collaboration)

Rowley also suggests that online marketing is critical to all businesses because of its 24-hour availability, global access, multimedia capabilities, interactivity and engagement, integration features, and one-on-one or micromarketing opportunities. Often, the first step for many entrepreneurs to connect with their digital community will be to establish a personal brand first.

YOUR PERSONAL BRAND

According to Gary Vaynerchuk in his book *Crush It* (2009), one of the most foundational building blocks to an entrepreneur's success is "learning to navigate the digital waters of social marketing by promoting a personal brand around what you love the most."

Vaynerchuk believes that personal branding is just as important as business branding (especially in the beginning of a side hustle or start-up business) because the individual is seen before anyone ever knows what his or her business does. He encourages his readers to "embrace your DNA, be yourself, put out awesome content, and people will be interested in what you have to say."

Another reason your personal brand matters is because you can establish what Seth Godin (2012) describes in the *Icarus Deception,* as the assets that matter:
- Trust
- Permission
- Remarkability
- Leadership
- Humanity: Connection/Compassion/Humility
- Stories that spread

Godin explains that **trust and permission** are important because in a loud, competitive world the person who will obtain our attention is someone who we trust and who has earned it. He describes **remarkability** as, "it is almost always new and untested, fresh and risky." I see remarkability like "sandwich thins" versus regular bread or bagels. So often, when someone expresses a fear about a market being oversaturated; someone else points out how many types of bread are on the bread aisle. I have made a similar comparison myself with types of water, alkaline water, to be exact. However, Godin is saying that it is not just enough to offer what everyone else is offering, you still have to own it and make it your own, make it special. You have to take the risk to present the old in a new way or with your unique new voice. While **leadership** in itself is not a new concept, Godin's approach to it has a twist. **Leadership** in the modern world is about ushering in bold new revolutions and inviting others to risk the change on the other side of the status-quo; not only at work, but in life. Humanity is in the presentation of vulnerability and transparency that can be hard to create or achieve in world that lacks empathy and emotional intelligence. However, you can achieve both within your personal brands. One way to do this is by using **stories that spread.** This last concept is about sharing stories that resonate with the hearer the way beauty resonates in the eye of the beholder and is achieved most effectively through storybranding.

STORYBRANDING

Another vital element for online communication is the ability to utilize the power of the "storybranding" to create stand-out brands. Author Jim Signorelli (2014) describes storybranding as a technique to ensure that the true story is told in his book *Story Branding 2.0*. He further expands the definition as "a strategic process based on the belief that story structure, or how stories are formed, will enhance a brand's appeal."

It is critical for entrepreneurs to understand that in addition to running the components of their business such as administrative and operational tasks, they are also in charge of making sure their message is visible and the correct storybrand is being achieved in the online world.

Storybranding can be a great tool for rebranding what Jones (2012) refers to as a "comeback brand." A comeback brand is a brand that gets a lifeline, almost like a do-over. A brand that pulled this off was Old Spice. The company created comical advertisements that resonated with the young millennial crowd. For example one commercial said, "If your grandfather had worn it, you wouldn't exist." This commercial instantly taps into the viewer's imagination. The brand was sold to Proctor and Gamble in 1990, who rebranded Old Spice by expanding the product line and creating the memorable and laughable commercials featuring Terry Crews. Forbes refers to this type of branding as a partial rebrand: is for the business that is well established, yet needs to refresh or update its services, marketplace or identity. This version tweaks parts of the brand to reflect a new focal point, be it new product offerings or a more contemporary look. Regardless of what you call it, if you have a brand that needs to be breathed back to life your storybranding will be critical, crucial, and key.

CHAPTER 2
GREAT BRAND CHARACTERISTICS

APPLYING YOHN'S PRINCIPLES FOR GREAT BRANDS

Now, let's dig into significant factors for creating and maintaining great brands. There are many practitioners and scholars who are passionate and knowledgeable about brands. During my studies, I found Denise Yohn's book *What Great Brands Do* to be one of the most significant for foundational branding information. We are going to discuss the seven key characteristics that she shares, but I want to stress one of the most critical points that she makes in the book and give you examples from my personal experiences. This point is the emotional connection factor.

THE POWER OF EMOTIONAL CONNECTION IN BRANDING

In her book, Yohn (2014) discusses the importance of connecting with customers by sharing the story of Proctor &

Gamble's Pampers brand. In 1997, the brand was losing a significant component of its profit share to Huggies. During a focus group, the company learned that while they did have the driest diaper; that was not the most profound issue for mothers. The most critical concern for mothers was the babies having diapers that helped them sleep better which was essential for their overall health and development.

One modification that was made because of this revelation was changing the names of the diapers to show concern and acknowledgment of the children's development stages. As a mother, I remember this period very well. Huggies launched an advertising campaign for *Pull-Ups*, the potty-training pampers for toddlers. The campaign resonated with the toddlers as well as the moms. Twenty years later, I can still recall the jingle: "Mommy, wow! I'm a big kid now." Even though I purchased Pampers previously, I never bought the Pampers training pants called *Easy Ups*. When my grandson started potty-training six months ago, I still purchased *Pull-Ups*. Over two decades later, and the emotional connection that I made to *Pull-Ups* still holds true.

Similarly, in our household, I am partial to Method products. During one of our classes, I learned the story of how Method products were created, and I instantly loved them. If you are not familiar with the story two childhood friends Adam Lowry and Eric Ryan started Method, an eco-friendly cleaning supply company with aesthetic appeal. Before this duo, cleaning products smelled toxic and were tucked away in cabinets and under sinks. In a Slate article, Ryan says his idea was to bring a spa aesthetic into a formerly drab, industrial market. While some customers were certainly attracted by the idea of nontoxic, environmentally friendly cleaning products, most people just wanted soaps and sprays that didn't stink and that looked nice on the countertop.

As someone whose allergies were always ignited by harsh cleaners, and as a creative Method products were a win/win. Needless to say, I have been purchasing them ever since, and also introduced my oldest daughter and mother to them as well. However, my husband has an emotional connection to Pine Sol, the original brand. Therefore, he is not interested in any new or improved scent. His childhood memories of cleaning with his mom and grandma include that smell, so he is emotionally connected to Pine Sol and will not use any other type of cleaning products. These examples and Yohn's breakdown of the Pampers dilemma proves just how powerful emotional connection to products can be.

YOHN'S GREAT BRAND CHARACTERISTICS

Yohn (2014) explains that there are seven principles vital to create and maintain great brands. We will not discuss all of them, but here is the list:
- GREAT BRANDS START INSIDE
- GREAT BRANDS AVOID SELLING PRODUCTS

ACTIVATE

- GREAT BRANDS IGNORE TRENDS
- GREAT BRANDS DON'T CHASE CUSTOMERS
- GREAT BRANDS SWEAT THE SMALL STUFF
- GREAT BRANDS COMMIT AND STAY COMMITTED
- GREAT BRANDS NEVER HAVE TO GIVE BACK

Again, I do not expect you to read every book mentioned, but this one book I strongly urge you to read. We will not unpack all the components but they are all critical.

These principles are all essential for both the necessities mentioned by Rowley (2014) and Signorelli (2014). Yohn expresses that great brands "start inside" and begin with the customer experience because "a brand can't be just a promise; it must be a promised delivered." Yohn further explains the value of creating a brand toolbox for the business which includes executable action plans and touch points so that each person that works on that particular brand moves in strategic alignment.

The notion of the brand toolbox will be more critical the more individuals/employees work for an organization. Once a business grows and has contractors and staff, it is the combined responsibility of the team to execute the brand, and that will always be significantly impacted by the culture of the business and "great brands put culture first." The second principle of great brands is that they avoid "selling products." Yohn's example of Nike is still a very relevant one.

Most recently, Nike launched a campaign featuring Colin Kaepernick, and although it was met with some negativity, in the end, Nike emerged victorious in what Yohn describes as "linking products to emotions." Yohn explains that few other companies are as disciplined at prioritizing long-term customer relations over short-term relations through emotional connection.

Today's consumers expect for brands to inspire them, and not to sell to them. This principle leads into the third one, which is "great brands ignore trends." Nike is still a great example because instead of treating Kaepernick the same way as one of their largest customers (the NFL) they went against the trend of one of the largest sports organizations in the world and did what Yohn describes as taking "a proactive approach to anticipating cultural movements, instead of a reactive approach to chasing transitory trends." Yohn notes that identifying a power idea or concept before it is fully actualized is very different than a reactionary jump on the proverbial bandwagon. It is critical for companies to know what risks to take and not to take.

Continuing to analyze Nike's decision to hire Kaepernick to do the ad for its 30th-anniversary campaign was certainly risky. According to Cody and Goodwin (2018), the public reacted quickly with some customers posting videos of burning their Nike products and stocks dropping by 3 % initially. However, several days later, the products were more popular than ever, with retailers struggling to keep them on the shelves after a 31 percent jump in online sales. Sixteen days after the stock initially dropped, the company's stock actually reached a record high with the market value reportedly increasing by 6 billion weeks after the ad was released.

One "trend" that companies (large or small) will be dealing with in the modern age is taking risks. A 2018 Glassdoor survey reported that 60 percent of employees expect their employers to take stands on important social and political issues. Applying the principles from Yohn mentioned thus far, if taking a stand helps customers to be inspired and form an emotional bond to the brand, then it would be an appropriate stand to take. However, if a company takes a position on an issue because the issue is trendy or popular but would not rest well with that company's tribe-based brand, then it would not be wise to do.

Next, "great brands don't chase customers" because the business can compel their ideal customer or tribe member since the brand clearly articulates what it stands for, who it is for, and has created a brand position as a high-value brand. One way that this is done is through overdelivering and owning a specific attribute. For example, in the fast food industry Chick-fil-A comes to mind for many as the company that owns customer service within that particular market because of their second-mile service described by Yohn (2014). Chick-fil-A is actually also an example of the next principle by Yohn, which is "great brands sweat the small stuff."

Chick-fil-A's program of "Second Mile Service" raises the concept of customer service to literally religious heights. The "second mile" is a reference to the biblical counsel that "whoever compels you to go one mile, go with him two. The company spends more than $1 million annually sweating the small stuff: quarterly research gives every restaurant a two-page report that shows how it's performing relative to the brand standards and to the chain's top performers. This attention to detail has led to awards [such as] "Top Large Chain" in Zagat's fast food survey and "Top Restaurant Brand" in J.D. Power and Associates restaurant satisfaction study. As a result, Chick-fil-A never has a 2 for $2 sale on anything; they do not have to chase customers. Their customers are looking for them and are sad when the sought-after establishment closes on Sunday.

During the final pre-press stages of this book, I pulled it to add a very important branding lesson regarding Chick-fil-A. According to CNN, Popeyes released a statement on Tuesday, August 27th that "extraordinary demand" for the sandwich led the company to be sold out in just two weeks since its nationwide debut on August 12th. Popeyes projected inventory would last till the end of September but the craze, fueled by social media, caused demand to exceed supply.

The backstory, as reported by Vox:

> On August 12, Popeyes, a beloved Louisiana fried chicken chain now headquartered in Miami, debuted its new fried chicken sandwich. A week passed, and

mostly, the world went on. And then on Monday, Chick-fil-A —America's favorite restaurant, according to the American Consumer Satisfaction Index, for the fourth year in a row, despite its controversial political history —wrote a tweet. The tweet said: "Bun+Chicken+Pickles = all the [heart] for the original." It did not mention Popeyes. It was just listing the ingredients of the chain's core chicken sandwich and implied that their sandwich had come first. Chicken sandwich enthusiasts on Twitter were quick to take notice, and within a few hours, Popeyes —or rather, the advertising agency GSD&M, which oversees the chain's social media strategy —fired back with its pièce de résistance: a quote tweet, plus a low-key expression of concern: "… y'all good?" it asked.

Now that is where it became interesting, the article also lets us know that after these two tweets a Pandora's box was opened on social media:

With that, the war was on, and everyone from passionate lay chicken enthusiasts to chicken professionals was weighing in. The conversation on Twitter, fueled by Black Twitter in particular, clustered around the hashtags #ChickenWars, and #ChickenSandwichWars, and the less combative, more descriptive #ChickenSandwichTwitter. Apex Marketing Group, an advertising consultancy in Michigan, released a report estimating that Popeyes received $23.25 million in free advertising, according to Reuters.

Now there are a couple of lessons to be learned. First, strategy for a brand is just as important as having a quality product. Popeyes is out of sandwiches which has left their customers angry and annoyed. Meanwhile, Chick-fil-A is still selling their "original sandwich" just as they were before the Popeyes sandwich craze started. Strategy focuses on details, and that is something that Chick-fil-A does consistently.

In other words, the details matter or as Yohn phrases it, "brand expression is in the details." The company's commitment to details is felt in the consistency of the food quality, preparation, and customer service, and the attention to those details are intentional and not accidental. This concept is an example of the necessity of detail-intentionality for building a great brand. These details are required to achieve the following brand principle "great brands commit and stay committed.

Finally, great brands "never have to give back" because generosity is a part of the fabric of the brand identity. In the same way, an increasing number of employees expect employers to take stands on important issues, 87 percent of consumers believe businesses should place at least equal emphasis on social interests and business interests. These beliefs explain why social entrepreneurship is on the rise.

The same aforementioned study illustrates that 76 percent of consumers in 2012 believed that it was acceptable for brands to support good causes and make money at the same time. If brands are created with this concept in mind, then the organizational values contain community initiatives that are already making a difference in the lives of others, so there is no need to launch elaborate empty "giving back" campaigns (Yohn, 2014).

Yohn's seven brand constructs are essential in building a lasting brand. Applying these constructs along with the social media messaging and emotional connection between brands and their tribes and audiences is non-negotiable for start-ups creating brands that can stand the test of time. These brand components showcase companies that are both profitable and are thriving within the market because they have established a connection with their audiences that demonstrates care and emotional intelligence are solving a pain point of their tribe or both.

In order to do this we must have a thorough understanding of tribes and audiences, we discuss that next in Chapter 3.

CHAPTER 3
TRIBES, SUPER FANS, & AUDIENCE = MEANINGFUL BRANDS

You may have heard this word a lot, but still be wondering, what is a tribe? Well, I am so glad you asked. This chapter will provide an in-depth discussion, but first, I must provide a full disclaimer. I highly recommend that if you are truly interested in learning more about tribes that you read both *Tribes* by Seth Godin (2008) and *Super Fans* by Pat Flynn (2019). You will see why, as we continue.

We can all agree that technology and the rise of the Internet have changed business branding and marketing in formerly unimaginable ways. Additionally, the widespread use of social media has created online communities that unite people previously bound by geographical constraints, and the members of that online community are considered a tribe. The tribe represents a collective of like-minded individuals who are unified by mindsets fueled across that specific online landscape and maintained by that particular leader (Godin, 2008). The rise of these types of communities and online leaders has changed the way the individuals and celebrities construct personal brands and the way that large corporations market and carry out their customer relations practices. Please note, a tribe is different from your network. I was reading a popular blog that described a tribe as "a group which includes peers, business associates, friends, family, and acquaintances." The only challenge with this is while you know the people in that group there is no way to be sure if you share what Godin (the Tribes' expert) describes as "like-minded individuals who are bound by common interest and generally led by one leader (occasionally more)." To date, Godin's book defines the tribe and its importance more succinctly than any of its competitors. For anyone who wants to more information on the tribes' concept, I highly recommend that you read the book in its entirety. I read it for a book report in graduate school, and it completely revolutionized my thinking about how leaders should be communicating with their followers.

Godin defines a tribe this way: any group of people, large or small, which are connected to one another, a leader, and an idea. According to Godin, tribes are a powerful force of influence and change; thus, marketers and other professionals should learn to tap into the potential of forming and leading tribes. Tribes are built by building messages and stories that are new, exciting, and relative to the members of that tribe. Additionally, tribes are facilitated by a leader or leaders that are committed to growth and change. This group is bound by their shared interest and method of communication. The opposite of a tribe is a crowd. Godin describes it this way, "A crowd is a tribe without a leader. A crowd is a tribe without communication. Most organizations spend their time marketing to the crowd. Smart organizations assemble the tribe."

Assembling tribes and creating super fans is what I would like to encourage each of you to do, but if you are not there yet, that is okay. I want you to get a basic knowledge of what tribes and super fans are, and then we will dive into a concept that may be more familiar with; which is audience. Just keep reading, I promise you, it will be worth it.

SUPER FANS: THE NEXT LEVEL TRIBE

Before we discuss audience, I want to share some information with you regarding another trending marketing concept. Author Pat Flynn will have released the book *Super Fans* by the time this book is printed. I had the privilege of experiencing the Super Fans presentation live when he was the keynote speaker in 2018 at the Social Media and Marketing World Conference hosted by Social Media Examiner. Flynn's "super fan" concept is like tribes on steroids.

He shared with us the super fans are not created overnight, but they are created by the moments that you create for them.

ACTIVATE

Essentially it is your job to turn your casual audience into an engaged audience. The goal is for them to feel your humanity, become your friend, and then your fan. Flynn points out that is crucial to get them to cheer for you. This happens by putting personality into your brand, giving them attention, and making them feel like they belong to whatever you are creating. He explained that one of the best examples of this was the Lego brand. That the physical toy was plummeting in a digital age and the company was $800 million dollars in debt in 2003. By 2018, the company's worth was $150 billion. The Lego brand was resurrected by a lot of creative and innovation additions such as Meet-Ups for adult fans of Lego, ideas.logos.com which a website where the Lego community can share their creation, submit new Lego ideas, shop, and enter contests.

There is also a Lego Idea conference which according to its website: "invites thought leaders, practitioners, researchers, government representatives and social innovators to share their insights on new ways of learning that will equip and empower children to become creative, engaged, lifelong learners. Each LEGO Idea Conference features some of the most inspiring and influential speakers on topics related to learning, education and early childhood development."

Flynn also lets the audience know that Lego allows individuals to be "certified members" that membership includes factory tours (behind the scenes footage) and special bonus content. He showcases them as a company that is doing a great job at securing their future by the steps that they are taking present day. He closed the keynote challenging each one of us to ask ourselves the question daily: "Have you earned a fan today?"

This is a question that I want you to ask yourself as you are building or rebuilding your personal brand. Because tribes and super fans are created because they are following a person who is offering solutions to his or her problems or is providing an emotional feel-good, inspirational encounter that they the individual cannot get anywhere else.

Over the last fifteen years, I have been working with individuals, small businesses, churches, and mid-sized non-profit organizations in the areas of communications, branding, marketing, and administration. As an entrepreneur who helps build brands, I encounter many clients who seem to struggle with the same areas in their businesses. One of the most critical factors to each entity's success or failure is their ability to cultivate and retain their tribe, combine the use of social media and email marketing, and demonstrate emotional intelligence through the components of social entrepreneurship or demonstrating care for the greater good. I chose to dig deeper into building purposeful and profitable brands because if the trends continue, small businesses and solopreneurs will continue to grow. Hence, this topic will be necessary for those starting now and those who decide to launch in the future.

WHAT ABOUT MY AUDIENCE?

If you have been in business or corporate for any considerable amount of time, the words "tribe" and "super fan" may be brand new marketing concepts. And if you are still wrapping your mind around that, breathe easy, I am not finished yet. **Audience** is the term that you probably most associate with your demographics. I do not want you to throw this word away, as a matter of fact, it is still relevant, I just want to introduce it to you differently.

In 2018, a good friend a colleague, DeSheila Spann invited me to do a workshop on branding at the Financial Fortitude Summit at Wake Technical Community College in Raleigh, NC. The one-hour session led me to create a four-week online training called **Activate Your Brand Academy.** During Week 2, I shared with my class how we can identify our audience to build our tribe. Author Danny Ivy transformed my understanding of audiences in his book *Audience Revolution*. I combined his concepts with some information that I developed after reading *Tribes* and created the infographic below for my students. Audiences are most important for those of you who are not on a mission to lead a movement or for those of you who are just starting out who may not have anyone to engage with yet.

During the Brand Academy I encountered another group of entrepreneurs. This group were in the beginning stages of creating a brand that solved a unique set of problems for a specific group of people. While doing so, they were still figuring out their exact business model. If you find yourself in this category than this section was designed specifically for you.

IDENTIFY YOUR AUDIENCE—
BUILD YOUR TRIBE

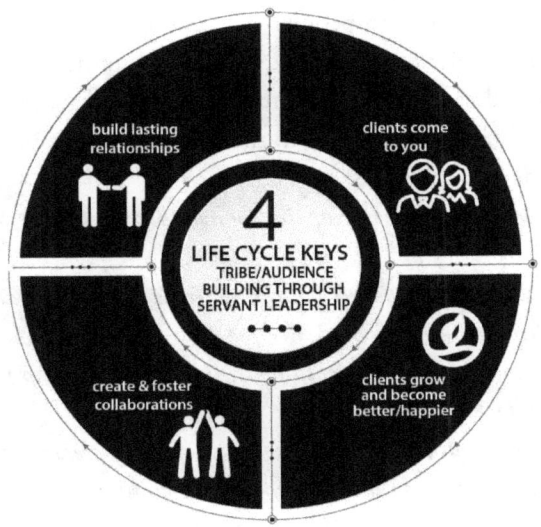

If you are truly going to identify your audience you must first understand what matters most to the people that you are called to *serve*. Both Danny Ivy and author Bernadette Jiwa hit upon a critical observation, although they express it differently. Ivy lets his readers know that they are not truly worthy to receive compensation until they first unlock a life cycle that creates change in the customer's life. I created the image above based on his observations.

Jiwa describes this same service to audience as "difference." She notes that 50 years ago the "focus of business was dominance" but today "it is not the person with best idea that wins, it's the person who has the greatest understanding of what really matters to people." She has 10 Characteristics of Difference Thinkers. You have a budding number of lists in this book already, so for the same of time, I will share the ones that are the most applicable to the audience discussion:

Difference thinkers:

- *They have a clear sense of the change that they want to make in the world.*
- *They watch what people do and don't just believe what people tell them.*
- *They make products for customers, instead of trying to find customers for their products.*
- *They work hard to change how people feel, by creating intangible value that gives them an emotional point of difference.*
- *They practice empathy because they care enough to make an impact.*

One of the reasons I opted to share this information with you is because Jiwa teaches us how to think differently about the audiences we serve. She suggests that the businesses that last in the future will be those that "invest time today to work out how to bring products and service to their market that show they understand the wants, needs and unexpressed desires of their customers."

When I was re-starting my business, I did not have a lot of money for expensive online courses. I stumbled across a young lady named Regina Anaejionu also known as @ByReginaTV. She did a segment on meaningful brands that ties in nicely with the *Four Life Cycle Keys of Tribe/Audience Building.*
Creating a meaningful brand that is humanized (with your personality), vital, useful, quality, and purposeful requires four components:

1. Define your Brand (Give it interest)
2. Give it Friends, Companions (Discover your friends, best audience)
3. Development a Content Plan (Blog, Email, Audio/Video Strategy, Social Media)
4. Design your brand (Give it face, dress, identity)

Defining your brand and giving it friends is all about audience. The people that you are uniquely qualified to serve and more importantly that you want to serve. Successful online marketers often share similar content in a way that is unique to their background and their story. Two marketers Marie Forleo and Nicole Walters both emphasized that the path to success was to clearly identifying who you wanted to support and help and that the surest way to failure was to focusing on the money that you wanted to make.

If we are honest there are many ways for us to make money and there is nothing wrong with that, it just can't only be about a profit. Now, let's be clear, we all need income. We all need to be able to pay our bills, but if you are only building a brand to produce profit you have already set yourself up to fail.

The key is to focus on making a difference. In Ivy's book Audience Revolution he shares some valuable gems on this subject matter. First, you make a difference by establishing connection with your audience. This connection is about gradual increased intimacy. Remember when you started dating your significant other? It would have been weird to walk up to them and tell them that you have been watching them and you think that they are the one, so you would like to introduce them to your parents. Well, for any normal person, that would see a little psycho and that person would most likely get away from you as quickly as possible. Well, connecting with an audience has similar steps to building most healthy relationships. It starts with shared interest and how you make the other person "feel." If you bring them joy, answer a problem, or help them see life with a little more clarity; they are more likely to want to keep you around. That is how it starts in the business world as well. You are sharing content with your audience (for free) because you just want to help. You are uniquely qualified to help them avoid pitfalls or struggles that you have faced and overcome. Instagram influencer Cici Gunn (also known as @ theSixFigureChick) says free information should be "what" information, while "how to do it" should be your paid content. The highest elevation of your purpose is being able to solve problems for people at a profit. There is truly no greater joy than getting paid for something that you love to do. Ivy shares Gunn's sentiments. You must take your audience into paid content because as Ivy declares: "cost and commitment go together." There is only so much value on free, your goal should be to give people enough free information for them to recognize the value of your time/product/service and establish that you have something to offer that is worth an investment. More importantly, it helps people take you and your product seriously. With this information in mind you should be ready to select or redefine your business model. In the Activate Brand Academy we share these **four business models**:

1. Product-based (People who sell products)
2. Service-based (People who provide services)
3. Content-driven (People who writers/publisher/create content/blog)
4. Voice-driven (People who speaker/provide trainings/ create podcasts & videos)
5. Informational Track: inform or educate on one or more related areas
   A. Inspirational Track: share inspiration/motivation in one or more areas

B. So after you have worked hard to put your audience first, create difference, provide quality content through one of these four business models the next step is to build your business model through the lens of servant leadership. Servant leadership unlocks a life cycle that leads you to create significant impact by changing the lives of those within your audience. Next, it unlocks the sweet spot of empathy and intimacy that lead to connection, care, and in-depth transformation. By focusing on the activities that you love and providing high inspiration you create abundance which increases your income by allowing you to be able to charge premium rates. Look back at the Life Cycle Key chart. When your clients come to you and they become happier and their lives get better this creates and fosters collaborations and a since of community (which ultimately creates your tribe and your engaged super fans). The cumulation of all these activities leads to the creation of lasting relationships.

I cannot stress enough the power of healthy, well-built relationships. Almost every long-term client that I have was introduced to me by word-of-mouth. I served at my last church for almost a decade, I have known my current beautician for almost a decade, and almost every client that I have was introduced to me by a person that has known be for at least five years. Relationships matter. If you are going to connect with an audience, build a tribe, and create super fans you must go the extra mile and learn the people that were designed to serve and take strategic action to reach them.

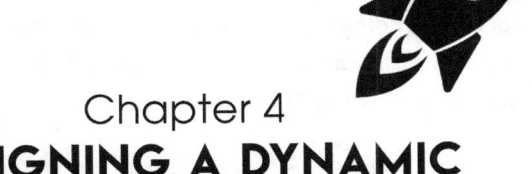

Chapter 4
DESIGNING A DYNAMIC CUSTOMER EXPERIENCE

To ensure the business brand that is being created can survive and thrive in the digital world, entrepreneurs need to **build a dynamic customer journey**, according to Solis (2013). The ingredients for forming a compelling customer journey or experience are outlined below.

First, you must institute the "**A.R.T.**" of Engagement.

A.R.T. =
Actions
Reactions
Transactions

These are the three necessary ingredients required to design an experience that creates an inspirational and emotional bind while providing exceptional value and solution-oriented concepts.

Next, it is essential to understand the importance of "social psychology," which is a dominant factor in how people perceive, earn, and spend social capital. Solis (2013) refers to them as the Six Pillars of Social Commerce:

Social Proof—This concept involves following the crowd and soliciting and accepting advice from family and friends regarding a digital purchase.

Authority—This attribute includes individuals, not only limited to celebrities and influencers with massive followers but also includes shopper reviews. Recent findings report that "77% of shoppers use reviews to make a decision."

Scarcity—minimal or short supply of an item drives exclusivity; the more limited or less available a product or service becomes, the higher it becomes in value to the consumer.

Liking—Commonly referred to as L.K.T. (like, know, trust) are factors that build bonds and establish trust; creating a brand that consumers like and trust is the best way to get followers across social media channels to buy from that business.

Consistency—Consistent brands rule, so entrepreneurs should build brands understanding that 62% of shoppers are brand loyal.

Reciprocity—Pay it forward; the same way great brands never have to give back (Yohn, 2014) because they are always giving, and superstar networkers are constantly giving; online brands should be benevolent.

The six pillars illustrate how essential it is for new businesses to be known for giving and providing value. Often companies use the "value opportunity" of exchanging their free information as lead magnets. A **lead magnet** is an incentive that marketers offer to potential buyers in exchange for their email address or other contact information. **Lead magnets** usually offer a piece of digital, downloadable content, such as a free PDF checklist, report, eBook, whitepaper, or video. The use of lead magnets should not only be a way to entice an individual to give his or her email address. The point is to be recognized as a trustworthy, giving brand that is creating a desirable experience that customers so that customers will want to return.

A giving brand is intentional about providing information that solves a pain point for that individual. It is critical to be viewed as someone who is providing value and not only someone who is continuously attempting to peddle goods and services. Let me give you an example.

Before taking media communications courses on the undergraduate level, I used to think of commercials as the annoying advertisements between the shows. After completing that coursework, I understand that shows are, in fact, the content between the advertisements. Applying this revelation to digital marketing means that social channels and brands that only advertise are displaying the annoying commercials without the "show content" that everyone tunes in to see. So, without content that provides value, whether that is humor, educational, resourceful, or even a discount off a product or service, the brand will fail to attract or retain consumers and prove incapable of creating tribes or a loyal fan base. So when you are creating social media content, make sure that you are providing content in between your ads and events. It will be nearly impossible to retain followers if you do not give more than you take. So if you have an event or product launch that you will be posting about frequently, you should also be increasing your free value content so that your viewers find value on your pages.

Solis has revealed the elements each brand should use when constructing a dynamic customer journey. Applying these will also aid with the next suggested strategy involving **content development using visual storytelling for social media channels**. Walter and Gioglio (2014) define visual storytelling as "the use of images, videos, infographics, presentations, and other visual platforms to craft a graphical story around crucial brand values and offerings. The popularity of visual storytelling has increased with the evolution of social media channels and platforms. Online posts that include photos and albums receive from 120 to 180 percent more engagement than posts that only contain text.

Visuals are essential for all facets of online business. Research from *Billion Dollar Graphics* reported that "46.1 percent of people discern a company's credibility based on their website design" and *MDG Advertising* shared that 67 percent of consumers consider clear, detailed images to be very important and carry more weight than the information, product description, and customer ratings. These statistics speak to the extreme value of images in brand evaluation and consumer decision-making. Here are the types of images that brands should use for visual storytelling, according to Walter and Gioglio (2014):

- Photography
- Graphs and drawings
- User-generated images
- Collages
- Images with text overlays: captions, quotes, and stats
- Word photos

These types of images are vital in providing what the authors describe as the 5-L approach to helping an audience or tribe connect emotionally with their brand. The 5-L looks like a pyramid. The bottom layer is a "lack of knowledge. The client moves from the "lack of knowledge" to "learn[ing] about the brand." Next, the client moves to "like" the brand, then the client "loves" the brand and the topic of the pyramid grows to the peak of emotional resonance, which is becoming "loyal" to the brand. See the image below.

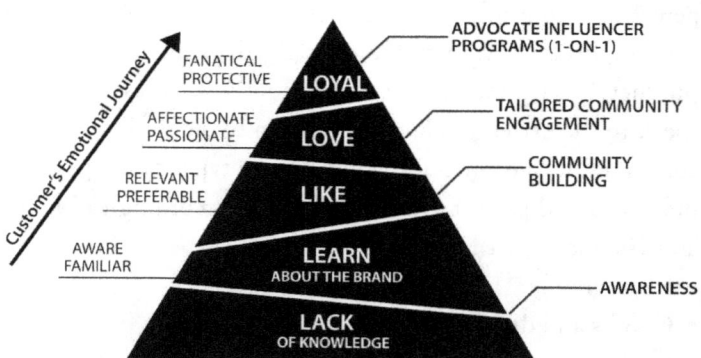

CUSTOMER-BRAND RELATIONSHIP MODEL | BASED ON ORIGINAL DESIGN CREATED BY @BRANDERATI P.26—WALTER & GIOGLIO (2014)

Once the brand has achieved brand loyalty through the A.R.T. of engagement, social psychology, and delivering visually compelling social media content, the next step is to foster and retain that brand loyalty by transforming consumers into fans of the brand. One way to drive brand fans is to provide them with multiple ways to stay connected to the business brand.

According to Jan and Kunz (2012), creating brand fans is done through a theoretical framework consisting of three zones: "gratification, participation, and customer-brand relationship." The brand's consumers are transformed into fans when their most prominent needs are met, which include "a content-oriented area based on information being delivered; a relationship-oriented area based on [positive] social interactions with others; and a self-oriented area where an individual need such as status achievement is met." The process, in summary, includes establishing a brand that meets a need of gratification in an individual or relational context; providing opportunities that create relationships and engagements between other brand users, and responding to consumers positively that creates meaningful dialogue, thus establishing a tribe leader/follower dynamic.

Practitioner Pat Flynn explains that, "Superfans are not created overnight; they are created by the experiences that you create for them." Experiences are created and maintained through the creation of strategic social media content. Kilgour, Sasser, and Larke (2015) explain that social media is a participatory medium and must be managed properly. They note that what is said is equally as important as who is saying it and that "corporations need to produce and curate content that fits the social environment, contributes to the social media community, and encourages user-generated content." Understanding how to create an overall strategy that has multiple touchpoints is critical in achieving social brand success. To ensure that the social media channels are updated with the type of content described in detail above, it is helpful to use the aid of a social media scheduler.

Two of the most popular schedulers that allow the scheduling of multiple social media networks are *Buffer* and *Hootsuite*. Beck (2018) compares the two, and they rate relatively the same overall, even though both have their strengths and weaknesses. Whichever one is selected will aid in maintaining a consistent social media presence, creating content and placing the text, photos, videos, and other elements in the scheduler. However, some components cannot be scheduled and require the diligence of the entrepreneur to ensure that there are authentic posts and interactive features such as live video as well.

Last, to fully implement an engaging customer journey, it is necessary to create a marketing and online strategy that involves the following components, according to Anaejionu (2013):

- Lead Generation (method to gain potential customers and get subscribed to your email list)
- Lead Conversion (system turn prospects into actual clients)
- Website Development (the digital business home that provides vital information regarding the company's brand)

- Creating a podcast, blog or vlog to increase search engine optimization and give customers another way to interact with the business brand
- Create monthly social media content using visual storytelling and a detailed customer experience plan (using the selling points outlined by Solis).

Your marketing and online strategy should be created with the A.R.T. of engagement in mind:

ACTIONS

The actions that you will need to take to build and maintain your audience; which include: creating social media content, useful information; and other channels to connect your content to your audience including, but not limited to podcasts, vlogs, blogs, and your website.

REACTIONS

It is not enough to merely exist within the digital world; you must foster engagement. Pat Flynn (2019) describes this process as an inverted pyramid (the large part of the triangle at the top with the point at the bottom). The inverted pyramid is divided into four sections (see image below). From top to bottom, the list is traffic, subscribers, sales page, and customers. The inverted triangle also functions as a sales funnel, and the reactions at each level create your overall customer journey.

RELIGIOUS NON-PROFIT REACTION PYRAMID

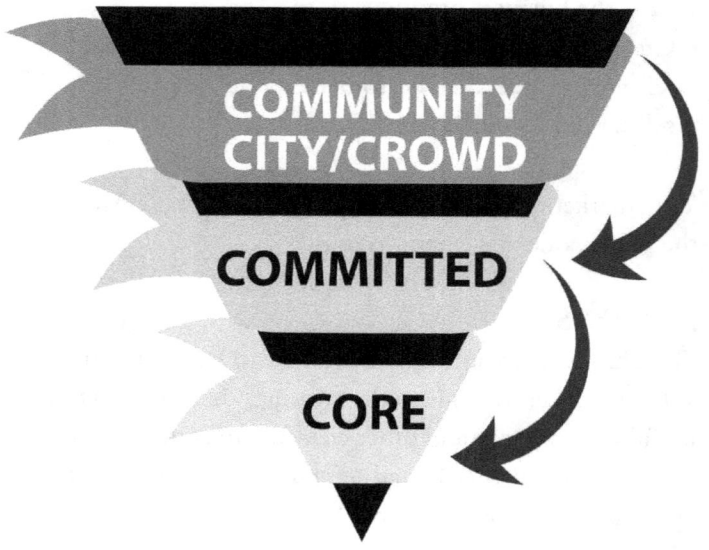

Each level generates a new level of engagement. The engagement level determines whether a customer continues on the journey and into a relationship your business or whether they abort or discontinue it. Let me give you an example of what this looks like, by giving you an inverted triangle of another organizational type.

One of the organizational types that I work with the most are religious non-profits or churches. I have over 20 years of volunteer, contract, and full-time staff experience in this particular area. All churches have attendees from their city and community, which church leaders associate as being the "crowd." These individuals attend church sporadically or on special occasions; such as weddings, funerals, Mother's Day, Easter, and New Year's Eve service.

The next level are considered the "committed." These are people who are committed to attending services monthly or weekly. These people are members of that particular church.

Finally, we have the "core." These are the people that are responsible for the operations of the church, including all leaders, staff, and volunteers. The goal of almost every church is to increase the reactions of each group, which means having the ***city/community/crowd*** people step up their reactions and become a ***committed*** member of the church, and to motivate committed members to become a part of the ***core***. This happens through the transactions of experience, which will discuss next.

TRANSACTIONS

In our church example, the transactions that occur must have relational impacts. There are multi-touch points that create the overall A.R.T. experience. The invitational social media post or video is a touchpoint. The user-generated content from other attendees is another touchpoint. Having designated parking spaces for first-time guests, having friendly greeters, and a welcoming children's ministry are a few of the vital transactions that create the relational currency that contributes to an incredible and dynamic customer/parishioner experience. These elements are the transactions that move people from the exterior of property to the pew, so to speak. However, getting people from the pew to participating through the giving of their time, talent, or treasure requires transactions which produce connections. These connections typically occur through friendships and relationships that invite other to serve and cease from merely being served. It is often the human capital transactions that are responsible for the step up from committed to core. Providing opportunities for others to learn and lead is paramount in these types of organizations.

This model works the same way in business. You, as the business owner, must create content that leads to actions, reactions, and provides transactions that create the types of experiences that are shared and grow your customer base. Now that we have discussed the importance of designing an optimal customer experience, let's talk about activating your brand and business.

SECTION II
ACTIVATE YOUR BRAND

CHAPTER 5
ACTIVATE YOUR BRAND

First, I want to make one thing abundantly clear. I am writing this book for individuals who still work their 9a-5p or 4p-11p or 12a-8p shift jobs as well as those who are full-time business owners. I am not telling anyone that you need to rush off and quit your job. I believe that the best time to build a business is when you do not have to be entirely dependent upon that business income to eat.

I believe that side hustles are the new job security and that businesses unlock the doors to financial freedom quicker than almost any other path. Financial freedom looks very different for every person, so some of the ways that I define it are:
- The freedom to design your schedule.
- The freedom to walk away from a job that mistreats you.
- The freedom to create extra income.
- The freedom to pay yourself what you are worth.
- The freedom to retire earlier.

These freedoms create increased opportunities, such as:
- extra funds for a vacation
- income for additional help (such as nannies, house cleaners, or landscapers)
- money to assist in eliminating looming debts such as medical bills, credit card debt, and student loans.

These are the types of freedoms that increase your quality of life, which is a form of self-care. Some people are stressed because while they have enough money to pay their bills, they do not have enough money for an incredible quality of life.

I want to encourage you to birth the dream in your head, and the vision in your heart. If you have tried and failed, that is okay. It is time to dream again. It is time to take the lessons learned in the failure and flip them into victory. It is absolutely possible. Also, if you have a business that is thriving, but you want MORE, than keep reading this part of the book is going to bless your life.

PURPOSE

When I was in graduate school, I learned so many powerful concepts that helped me increase the profitability of my business. I wanted to share those concepts with you, and I put them in the first part of this book. I wanted you to understand what a brand was and the elements you needed for your business brand before I prompted to ACTIVATE it!

If you have more questions about the branding portion, I want you to contact me at info@activatedream.com. That is an email that I use for business owners and church/ministry leaders to contact me individually regarding the topics addressed in this book. I answer each one myself (not my assistant) so be patient with me because I receive a lot, but I will answer you. You must know that you are not alone in this process.

ACTIVATE MINDSET

Again, you may be working for someone else or be the boss. Regardless of what your position is, you must be clear that as the famed lyricist Redman would say, "It's time for some action." An activate mindset is ready to act. So, let's jump into activation.

DECIDE—

The very first step to activating your brand is to make a decision. Some of you a dream that has been locked in you so long, you are not sure it can be brought to life. Well, I came with the keys to release your dream out of dream JAIL. Often, jailed dreams are the result of people that are prisoners of the circumstances, situations, and challenges of life.

So let me pause for station identification and let you know that you are more than what you have been through and survived! One factor that can rob you from the activation of your first dream or from pursuing a bigger dream is fear. This fear is either the fear of failure or the fear of the past. Often, it can be a combination of the fear of past failure that has immobilized you to take steps to go forward in this new season. I encourage to decide to use the information that you learned in the first part of this book to give you the confidence to begin again or begin to go "bigger."

BECOME DISTRACTION INTOLERANT—

When I was pregnant with one of my daughters, I become lactose intolerant. I had to avoid dairy at all costs. At first, this was tough for me, because I loved cereal and milk. It was one of my favorite foods, but I decided that the effects of the milk on my body were not worth the momentary enjoyment of my Frosted Flakes. In the same way, you must realize that you are distraction intolerant when you are building a business brand. I remember when Netflix first came out, it was one of my chief distractions. I had to use the streaming service as a treat that I earned once I had unlocked one of my goals. If not, I found that I would waste valuable time that I could be using to increase my productivity. Now, I am not saying that you should never watch TV or stream your favorite show. I am saying that when you are frustrated with your finances or are serious about enhancing your quality of life, you cannot afford to be distracted.

I have seen too many people's destiny derailed by distractions, and I do not want that for you now. Let's be clear distractions come in many forms. Distractions exist on social media platforms, in political arguments, in holding onto relationships that are no longer healthy for you, and in staying in your comfort zone. I once worked with a dynamic business coach named Cherelle James that said, "What you tolerate is often the very thing that stands in the way of your success. So, in this season, be careful about what you tolerate and whom you tolerate. Sometimes people and situations keep from fully activating our brands, businesses, and dreams.

EVALUATE—

Every race has a starting point. Take some time for a personal and professional assessment. One of my favorite technological advances is GPS. I am one of those people that uses the GPS all the time. It helps me navigate traffic, teaches me shortcuts, and it gives me my time of arrival. However, the GPS must have two coordinates to produce a route. It must have your current location and your final destination. You can search and add stops along the way, but your starting point is a requirement. In the same way, you must pause to be able to receive the coordinates for your business brand planning.

Ask yourself:
- *Where am I?*
- *What will it take to achieve my goals?*
- *Can I do this alone or whom do I need to help me?*

MOTIVE CHECK—

If you are looking for a get rich quick scheme playbook, then this book will not help you. The tribe-based brand strategy is for those who are not only about the MONEY but are also trying to create a MOVEMENT. The truth is that I, like many other coaches and consultants, believe that everyone has a unique set of people that they are uniquely created to reach and impact. The good news about that is that you do not have to be on a mission to have 100,000 followers. You must be intentional about impacting the people that you are uniquely created to serve, help, and assist. I assure you, the profit part will come when you activate your purpose, and if you are committed to putting in the work required to manifest your dream. So many people get lost because they are seeking INCOME before IMPACT. However, some of the most successful people quietly put in work helping people in obscurity before they ever reached popularity or wealth.

EXPECTATIONS—

In order to succeed in activating your business you have to set proper expectations. Now, when it comes to others, I believe that you have to set expectations appropriately to guard your heart in a sense and maintain a life of peace. However, when it comes to setting expectations for your business I would like to share a few lessons from Grant Cardone's 10X Rule book:

First, write down your goals every day, and secondly, choose objectives that are "just out of reach." According to Cardone (2011), selecting goals that are "just out of reach" opens you up to your full potential, which can be used to fuel your action every day. In order to do this successfully, I suggest you start with the end of the mind. You do this by asking yourself these types of questions:

- ***How would I build this business if money were not an option?***
- ***What is the ideal location for my office, facility, or church to be located?***
- ***How many people do I need on my team and what is my plan to find and secure the best talent?***

Once you answer those questions, you can create your goals. Another tip from Cardone is to, "word your goals as though you have already accomplished them." I love that because it establishes expectations of victory in your mind, before you ever start. Moreover, it takes the fear out of getting started. For some of you that is the biggest obstacle to overcome to do the first thing or the next big thing for your business. You need to step out and start. Start now. Start today. Start right where you are. Start with what you have. You may not be able to see the entire path yet, and that is okay. Sometimes you find a vision, more often, VISION finds you. Vision is attracted to movement. It is time to activate, so don't wait another day!

CHAPTER 6
ACTIVATING YOURSELF

After accepting the ACTIVATE mindset, you will have to continually work to activate yourself and maintain a mentality of activation. Even after you have generated a level of success, there are always small attacks that happen to unsettle, distract, or delay your progress. It would be best if you fought them like a plague. Inevitably, there will always be children who disobey, times when parents disappoint, instances where relationships require more work, and seasons of life that are more difficult than others; but you must remain committed to your business and yourself. ***People are waiting for you to create an answer to their problem.*** That truly is what activation and leading your tribe-based business is all about: it is about you showing up to solve a problem that you are uniquely qualified to fix. You must never forget that ***you have been empowered and equipped to provide the antidote for the issues your clients and customers face***.

ACTIVATE

One way to initiate and sustain activation is through continuing education and constant motivation. Now, I do not want anyone to rush out and obtain a new degree (unless you feel you need it). When I say continuing education, I mean reading books, attending webinars and conferences, and maybe obtaining a certification or specialized training. One of the reasons that I list so much information from others in this book is to encourage you to read material from practitioners who are winning in areas where you need help. In my graduate studies program, I was surprised when the professors were assigning readings from Seth Godin, Gary Vaynerchuk, and Brian Solis, but it taught me a valuable lesson. The lesson I learned is that the information that the practitioners bring to the table is just as important as the academic theories. The knowledge works together. So if you are going to be a leader in your field, build a brand, and make a difference, you must read. Cardone (2011) stated that: "The average worker reads an average of one book a year and works an average of 37.5 hours per week. This same person makes about 319 times less money than the top U.S. CEOs, who claim to read more than 60 books per year." In summary, as we (Generation Xers) learned from the PSAs, "reading is fundamental."

Secondly, you must emerge yourself in motivation and inspiration. If you are reading this book and you are a Christian, I encourage you to listen to sermons from your favorite pastors. I also encourage everyone to find uplifting individuals, motivational speakers, YouTube channels to subscribe to, and positive social media channels to follow. You must develop a zero-tolerance policy when it comes to negativity. It is hard enough to build a brand, create a business, work on a ministry, without also having to fight forces of negativity. It is essential that you guard your inner circle and your mind gates. Some people cannot have a front seat in the rows of your life during this process.

One of the reasons is that anyone who called to do anything significant already battles with Imposter Syndrome. During an excellent webinar on Clarity of Purpose by Nicole Walters, she communicated that minorities and women battle with this mindset more than any groups. If you are wondering precisely what Imposter Syndrome is, it is the mentality that struggles to accept that you are good enough. This syndrome causes high levels of anxiety and stress, even with people who have achieved success and have worked hard at all levels educationally, professionally, physically, and relationally.

If you are someone who struggles with this, I would like you to consider Malcolm Gladwell's 10,000-hour rule, which states that anything you do for 10,000 hours you are an expert in that particular area. Now, it is highly debated by some scientists and professionals, but the overall point is valid. The more experience you have in something, the more efficient you become. Therefore, you must use your gifts, knowledge, and expertise to give you confidence that you are fully equipped to help meet the needs of others in a specific area.

The way that I overcame Imposter Syndrome is by replacing the people in my inner circle. A few years ago, I was asked what kinds of people I replaced them with, and this was my answer:

NINE TYPES OF PEOPLE YOU NEED

- **People who are loyal:** these are individuals that you can trust. When you are in a time of vulnerability and building, you don't need people who will steal your ideas or tell other people about your fears and lows. It is crucial for you to have people who will have your back.
- **People are honest:** these are individuals in your life who will tell you the truth in love. The key though, is finding people who truly speak the truth in love because the truth without love will create offense. However, everyone needs someone in his or her life who can lovingly provide constructive criticism and accountability.
- **People who truly support you:** you need your own cheerleaders. You need to have people in your life that will cheer you on when you are facing the storms of life. Those people are as refreshing as rain in a desert.
- **People who know the real you:** you need people with whom you do not have "fake it until you make it". These are people with whom you can be yourself, with no judgment.

- **People who are successful:** because high achievers and accomplished individuals are less likely to discourage your dream. These are the people who always have a story of someone who flipped defeat into victory and how you can do the same thing. These people have learned how to take the lessons from fail and win, and they encourage you never to give up!
- **People who add value to you:** these are individuals who give as much as they take. I'm often amazed at how many people keep takers in their lives just so that they will have someone around. I am not judging; as I have been there myself. Just know that when you release the leeches and the takers in your life, you leave room for God to bring people who can bring you gifts, and occasionally pick up the check. Do not delay your destiny due to dealing with life-draining takers.
- **People who look up to you:** someone needs the information that you already have. You are the answer that one of your friends or family members needs right now. You stay sharp when you are providing knowledge and information to others.
- **People who inspire you:** your "favorites" on your phone and your social media timeline need to be full of people who encourage you to get up every day and go higher! It is beneficial to have people with whom you can touch (such as the favorites in your phone) and people whom you admire from

afar (your social media influencers, motivational speakers, favorite preachers, game-changers) that motivate you on your worst days.
- **People who offset negative emotions:** generally, this role belongs to a good spouse, parent, or best friend. You need someone in your life that can talk you off the bridge or keep you from "giving someone a piece of your mind." Too many people have people who "hype" them up and instigate negative behaviors, such as violence or depression. Ultimately, it is beneficial to have people who are strong in areas that you are weak.

Now that you have learned about branding, tribes, creating your customer experience, the activation mindset for both you and your business, I would like to conclude by talking about idea implementation and business next steps.

CHAPTER 7

ACTIVATE YOUR BUSINESS 101:
BUSINESS SET-UP, IDEA IMPLEMENTATION, AND ACCEPTING PAYMENTS

One of the most critical elements of business is the process of taking a concept from idea initiation to implementation. The first thing that I want to point out to you is that because there is nothing new under the sun, it is not uncommon for two or more people to have the same idea. However that should not discourage you, because your unique interpretation or spin on the product or service can still become a profitable idea for you to create. The key is to take your time and decide what product or service that you can create that you do the best and that will generate the most income for you with as little overhead as possible. You want to do this because it is easier to establish yourself and your brand the more precise you are about exactly what you offer.

So please be mindful of the biggest traps for entrepreneurs starting out; the first being the temptation to offer as any products and services as possible. The second is to fail to describe your offers adequately. I strongly encourage you to create these columns a sheet of paper or in your journal and list all of the products/services you are considering creating.

Product/Service	Features	Solutions/Benefits	Cost/Pricing

Refer back to the chapter on audience while you are listing these, because your audience/tribe plays should be an essential consideration in what you create and how you offer it.

One of the biggest challenges I see in businesses is the tendency to create something that a business owner wants to sell versus something that his or her ideal client needs. I strongly encourage you to do your due diligence and test the products and services that you need with a beta group of participants that pay a lower price so you can see if this a good or service that is desired by your audience and to assess the ideal price point for this good or service.

The reason that I suggest you put in this level of work is because eighty percent of small businesses fail, and I want you to be successful. There are lot of reasons that the businesses don't thrive and a good portion is centered around the planning and strategies; or lack thereof. So we are going to give you a crash course in getting started and the types of professionals you will need to assist you in the process so that you can create a business that yields you a profit. The profitability factor is crucial, because if you are not making money than you have created a very expensive hobby for yourself!

Now, do not get me wrong. You are not creating a business to just make money; however, remember our financial freedom list? Well, that list is only realized if we create a profitable business that is fueled by your purpose and is making an impact in the lives of people whose problems are being solved by you. See, it is a win/win situation!

Alright, let's jump into the crash course—we will call is Activate Your Business 101.

BUSINESS NAME SELECTION

First, you must select a Business Name. There are a lot of factors when choosing a name, but here are a few to consider:

- **Keep it short and simple**—your name will drive all of your marketing materials; so short, but precise will always be best. Also, remember that your website domain, social media channels, and other promotional items will contain your business name.
- **Think global**—in our global economy, please keep your business name in mind as it will translate into other languages.
- **Name Check Research**—Check your name popularity and availability on your Secretary of State's website and the

U.S. Patent and Trademark Office. Also, do web searches to ensure that your potential name has not been used negatively or criminally in any way.

BUSINESS NAME PROTECTION*

There are several measures of protection for your business name.

- **Federal:** Register a federal trademark with U.S. Patent and Trademark Office
- **State:** Form corporation, LLC, or register a state trademark
- **County:** File an assumed name certificate at your county clerk's office
- **Digital:** Reserve your website domain and social media accounts

SELECTING A BUSINESS ENTITY*

The five most common types of business entities are:

- **Sole Proprietorship:** a person who is the exclusive owner of a business, without creating a separate entity. The owner is also entitled to keep all profits after tax has been paid but liable for all losses.
- **General Partnership:** this is also an unincorporated for of business that it similar to the sole proprietorship, except it includes two or more people.
- **Limited Liability Company:** this business type is a separate entity and it provides limited liabilities to its members/

managers, which protects the owners' personal assets.
- **Corporation:** this is a business type that can be owned by a single individual (in some states) while others require two or more entities. This business structure also safeguards the owners' assets and it provides many additional benefits. If you select this entity you may want to ask your accountant about S-Corporation type which protects against double taxation.
- **Non-profit Corporation:** Non-profits are formed similarly as corporations, but they are created for some type of public benefit and are eligible for tax-exempt status; which much be applied for under the IRS-code, section 501(c) (3).

OBTAINING YOUR EMPLOYER IDENTIFICATION NUMBER (EIN)

The EIN is the business equivalent to a social security number. You will need if you have to pay contractors or employers; and you also need it for applying for business credit and securing your business banking accounts. Even if you are just getting started, it is highly recommended that you start out separating your business and personal income. It makes it much easier for you and your accountant in the future.

Disclaimer: No one at Raindrop Brand or any of our companies are accountants or attorneys, so we encourage you to seek the counsel of these types of professionals if you need assistance in these areas. There are two accounting service brands that we follow and that have been recommended to us are Accuro Corporate Services: http://accurocorpservices.com and accounting firm led by Faith Bynum: http://www.faithbynum.com.

PAYMENTS

One of the most significant factors in the success of business now from when I started doing business in 2004 is the ease of obtaining electronic payments. It is easier than ever to receive money. A few ways to receive electronic payments:
- PayPal
- Venmo
- CashApp
- Square
- Stripe
- ApplePay
- Quickbooks

Quick note—If you are a non-profit organization, ministry, or church, please consider adding text-to-give options to your website giving. We live in a time where fewer people are writing checks and carrying cash so the easier it is to give to your organization the better. This also includes making sure your website and mobile giving is user-friendly.

Here are a few of the most popular ones:
- **Church Center**https://planning.center/giving
- **Giving Fuel** https://www.givingfuel.com
- **Push Pay**https://pushpay.com
- **Secure Give**https://www.securegive.com
- **Subsplash**https://www.subsplash.com
- **Tithe.ly**https://get.tithe.ly/church-giving

Some of the listed methods (for both profit and non-profit payments) are less preferred than others, so it is best to check with your accountant to set up a system that works for you both.

BUSINESS BRAND & IDENTITY

Your budget would be the biggest factor in the recommendation that I gave to you in regards to getting your logo, social media graphics, business card design, and other promotional materials designed.

Do-It-Yourself Branding Tools:
- **CANVA** is a simplified graphic-design tool website, founded in 2012. It uses a drag-and-drop format and provides access to photographs, vector images, graphics, and fonts. It is used by non-designers as well as professionals. The tools can be used for both web and print media design and graphics.
- **CREATIVE MARKET** is an online marketplace for community-generated design assets. The company sells graphics, WordPress themes, stock photography, and other digital goods for use by web creatives.

Graphics for Emails & Social Media
- CanStock Photo
- Unsplash (free)
- Flickr Creative Commons (free)
- Fotolia

ACTIVATE

- Creative Market
- Stocksy
- Pixabay (free)
- Canva (free)
- Pixlr (free)
- Pixelmator
- Istock

Branding/Design from Online Companies
- http://99design.com
- http://Fiverr.com
- http://Upwork.com

Hiring Raindrop Brand and Other Agencies for Branding/Design Services

Over the last few years, our company has been taking fewer branding clients. There are so many options available, which has made it difficult for people to see the value in hiring a company over an online service. I want to explain a few of the differences between hiring us or any design firm over an online brand.

First, we are going to start with the owner and do a marketing overview to be sure that we understand your goals, objectives, and audience. We are going to show similar work of past projects that demonstrate the quality and type of work that we do. Then we are going to work with our design and marketing team to produce your brand colors and a vector logo that can be scaled to any size. We also will deliver your logo to you in multiple format types so that it can be used everywhere from your website to a billboard. Also, we work with multiple designers so we select the one that is the fit for your business needs. Most other agencies, work similar to this as well. It is more expensive, you receive hands-on treatment of your product and updates by a dedicated project manager. Often, agencies can also take you the full-package offering from logo to website creation. When agencies do not staff all of the persons needed for the client they often contract parts to local agencies that give them discounted rates, which they pass on to the customers. Here are a few designers and web developers that we have active partnerships with:

- http://nonajaneco.com (Website)
- @brittanyoliverannis (Facebook, IG)
- http://www.mainlandcreative.com (Website)

COMPREHENSIVE DIGITAL STRATEGY: SOCIAL MEDIA CHANNELS AND EMAIL MARKETING

In Part I of the book, we discussed that social media alone was not enough to build your online brand. A complete strategy combines the use of both social media networks and email marketing to communicate and build engagement with your tribe-based brand.

There are a lot of social media and digital platforms available today. For the sake of time, I am going to share information about four platforms that are dominating the social scene for our clients: Facebook, Instagram, LinkedIn, and YouTube. Not to say that those are the only ones because Twitter, SnapChat, TikTok and many others are all relevant platforms. The four below are the ones that our clients are using the most:

Facebook: http://www.facebook.com
According to Statista, with 2.41 billion monthly active **users** as of the second quarter of **2019, Facebook** is the biggest social network worldwide. Gail Z. Martin (2010) likens Facebook to a global business-networking luncheon that's open 24/7. It is easy to share multimedia information, get involved in trending conversation topics, and connect with new prospects.

Here are some interesting stats as you are planning Facebook into your digital strategy:
- Only 51% of teens use Facebook (In order Teens use these platforms the most:
- You Tube 85%—Instagram 72%—Snap Chat 69%—Facebook at 51%—Twitter 32%
- India has the highest number of Facebook users in the world (at 300 million, the U.S. is in 2nd place with user numbers)
- 68% of Americans use Facebook second only to YouTube (73%) and the majority report using it online or on their

mobile device (Pew Research Center)
- 96% of Facebook users access it on mobile or tablet
- 74% U.S. Adults log on to Facebook daily
- 43% of users get their news from Facebook
- Users spend an average of 35 minutes a day on Facebook
- At least 3% of Facebook profiles are fake, about 88 million accounts were removed in 2018 following the safety concerns of the 2016 Presidential election
- 85% of Facebook videos are watched without sound
- Facebook videos and Live-streams are up to 8 billion views per day
- People spend 3x as much time watching a Live video than a pre-recorded one

Instagram: http://instagram.com

According to Oberlo, there are 1 billion monthly active **Instagram users**. **Instagram** is the most engaged network after Facebook. 71% of the billion monthly active **users** on the **Instagram** app are under the age of 35. Sprout Social reports some other interesting facts about Instagram that all business owners should keep in mind:

Nearly two out of every three adults aged 18-29 use Instagram.
- 80% of accounts follow a business on Instagram
- Not only that, but 200 million Instagrammers actively visit business profiles everyday.

- The best times to post daily on Instagram are weekdays between 10 a.m.–3 p.m.
- Video posts receive 38% more engagement than image posts
- Over 100 million photos are uploaded every day
- Instagram Stories now has 500 million daily active users and 1 out of 3 of the most viewed Stories are from businesses
- 68% of Millennials consume Stories on Instagram vs. 49% on Snapchat and 44% on Facebook
- Users spend 53 minutes a day on Instagram
- The platform gets 4.2 billion likes per day, Instagram has the highest engagement rate of all platforms, at about 2-7% of all posts.

LinkedIn

LinkedIn is often considered the professional business and networking channel among social media networks. It functions very differently than the other platforms. In March 2019, the network has 303 million active monthly users, 40% of which visit the site daily. 90 million senior-level influencers and 63 million decision makers use **LinkedIn**. 57% of companies had a **LinkedIn** company page in 2013. 46% percent of the social media traffic to B2B company sites is from **LinkedIn**.

Here are some facts that you may not know about this platform:
- Two professionals join LinkedIn every second
- 154 million American workers have LinkedIn profiles

(America has the highest number of profiles)
- 50 percent of Americans with a college degree use LinkedIn (average household income is $75,000 per year)
- Equally popular with women and men
- Highest age range is between users ages 25-49
- 57 percent of LinkedIn use is on mobile
- 45 percent of LinkedIn users are in upper management
- 3 million American jobs are posted on LinkedIn every month
- 2 million posts, articles and videos are published on LinkedIn every day
- Posts with images get twice as many comments
- Video posts are 5 times more likely to get comments
- 91 percent of executives rate LinkedIn as their first choice for professionally relevant content
- 30 million companies have LinkedIn profiles
- InMail has a 300 percent higher response rate than email

YouTube

Martin (2010) describes You Tube as the "granddaddy of video-sharing sites." YouTube is the world's **second largest search engine** and **second most visited site** after Google. So if you are not on YouTube you, do not want to wait any longer. I had the opportunity to hear Sean Cannell of Think Media do a presentation on You Tube at Social Media Marketing World in 2018. Here are his suggestions for getting started:

Activate

- Start with end in mind
- Pick a topic (ideally trending or polarizing)
- Don't overthink it
- Outline your Content
- Pre-plan Questions for Interviews
- An Ideal video is 12-18 minutes, but ultimately to make content long as needs to be but short as possible
- Continue to promote your replays

Cannell continued his presentation encouraging the audience to "Go Live" on You Tube. He suggested that you let people know when you were going to be live, and remind them again before you start. Cannell also advised everyone to complete your title, description, tags and thumbnail BEFORE you go live. After your live video is over, you should optimize the video after the stream is over. Cannell shares his equipment list at Kit.com/seancannell, if you need assistance with equipment purchases.

To conclude this section I will share a few You Tube stats with you:

YouTube User Stats:
- The platform has over **1.9bn logged in monthly users**.
- **6 out of 10 people** prefer online video platforms to live TV.
- By 2025, **half of viewers under 32** will not subscribe to a pay-TV service

- In an average month, **8 out of 10** 18-49 year-olds watch YouTube
- In 2015, 18-49 year-olds spent 4% less time watching TV while **time on YouTube went up 74%**
- On mobile alone, **YouTube reaches more 18-49 year-olds** than any broadcast or CABLE TV network
- You can navigate YouTube in a total of **80 different languages** (covering 95% of the Internet population)
- The platform has also launched in **over 91 countries**

You Tube Usage stats:
- YouTube is the **2nd most popular social media platform** with 1.9bn users.
- On average, there are **1,000,000,000 mobile video views** per day
- 400 hours of video are uploaded to YouTube every minute
- Users watch over **1 billion hours** of YouTube videos a day, **more than Netflix and Facebook video** combined
- **70%** of YouTube views come from mobile devices
- The average mobile viewing session lasts **more than 40 minutes**
- 81% of US parents use **YouTube to find content for their children**.
- 51% of Users use the site as an instructional resource to teach them how to do something that they have never done before

- Searches of "how to" videos on YouTube are **growing 70% year on year**

YOUTUBE MARKETING STATS
- The number of channels earning six figures each year on YouTube has **increased by 40%** year on year
- Among millennials, YouTube accounts for **two-thirds of the premium online video** watched across devices
- In 2018, the **95% of the most watched videos were music videos**

Email Marketing—Overview
One of the best email marketers of our time is a guy named Ryan Deiss, who is the founder of Digitalmarketer.com. In his book Invisible Selling Machine (2015), he shares five phases of invisible selling, which is an in-depth explanation of his email marketing strategy. His book illustrates this strategy on a process map. You can get more information on it at http://digitalmarketer.com. For the sake of this overview on email marketing, I have created an infographic for you to see the steps clearly. Most digital marketers have some version of strategy. Often, it is shown using a funnel graphic, because these are the same concepts used in many of the funnel plans as well.

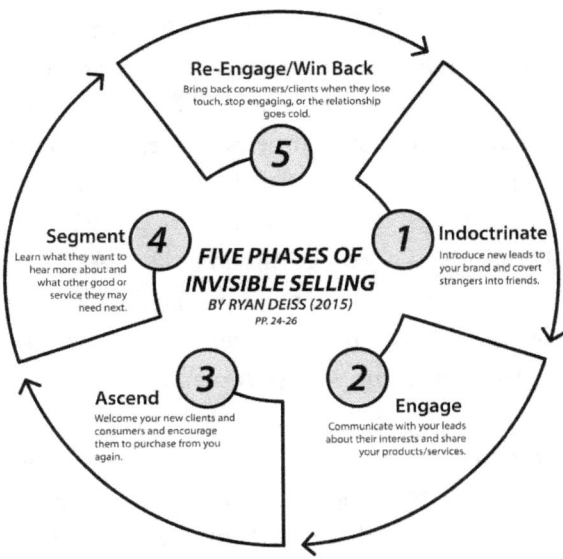

As you can see, the first step is to **indoctrinate** your leads to your brand and to convert strangers into friends. I have had the opportunity to hear Ryan Deiss speak live and he shared that this first step is the one that brands mess up the most frequently. He illustrates the importance of not skipping this first step. Deiss suggested with the crowd that if anyone was asked to get married on the first step, most people in the room would be horrified and never want to see that person again. The crowd laughed and unanimously agreed. He quickly followed up by telling the audience that is a picture of what marketing looks like without **indoctrination** and **engagement**. Stages 1 and 2 should result in someone liking your brand enough and trusting your brand enough to make a purchase. From that point, you should welcome them in as a part of your "brand family" and then they should be prompted to **ascend** (stage 3) to become a part of your tribe. At that point, the customer should be introduced to **segmentation** (stage 4) which informs them of other goods or services that you offer. Now, after stage 4 you would either continue to **re-engage** them or **win them back** (step 5), if they stop opening your emails or if they seem to no longer be engaging with your brand.

Email List Tools

If you want to send attractive looking emails, you will need a comprehensive HTML email client and some great graphics. You can also opt to send more "normal-looking" emails directly from your regular email platform. Here are some options to get you started:

- MailChimp (with a free plan or paid plan)
- MailerLite
- AWeber
- Constant Contact
- Campaign Monitor

Email Marketing = Passive Income

You may have heard the term passive income, but not be entirely sure how it works. Passive income is money earned in a way that requires little to no daily effort to maintain. Blogger and Wealth Expert Chris Hogan shares four reasons to consider a passive income business, which looks similar to our earlier lists of activating your business:

- Increases your wealth-building plan
- Creates an opportunity to retire early
- Protects you from a complete loss of income if you lose your job
- Provides an additional source of income when you're no longer able to work or if you outlive your retirement fund

One of the most important facets of passive income is mastering email marketing. The nuances of which emails to send, exactly how to word them, when they should be sent, and how many to send could be an entire book on its own. My goal in writing Activate was to get you started in the right direction with all the tools at your disposal to work your side hustle, be entirely in business for yourself, or increase the reach of your ministry, or grow the revenues of your non-profit organization. Two of the books I highly recommend if you are ready to get started with email marketing are *Invisible Selling Machine: 5 Steps to Crafting an Automated Evergreen Email Campaign that Literally Makes Sales While You Sleep* by Ryan Deiss (2015) and *Launch: An Internet Millionaire's Secret Formula to Sell Almost Anything Online, Build a Business You Love, and Live the Life of Your Dreams* by Jeff Walker (2014). These two books will give you the tools, information, and resources needed to use email marketing effectively, which is often the most important factor in creating passive income.

BONUS CHAPTER
TWO ESSENTIAL LISTS FOR BUSINESS OWNERS AND ACTIVATE HELP

I trust that this book has been insightful, informative, and inspirational. I am passionate about helping people start businesses and activate their dreams (no matter how big or small) because I am a living, breathing, example of how beneficial a business can be not only for the creator, but for the creator's family, as well as the people who the business serves.

When I first became serious about leveling my business up I was exposed to two lists that I kept in notes on my computer which I shared with my clients time and time again. Now, I realize that I have provided a bunch of lists in this book. That is why we refer to it is as mixtape for your business! It has the best "hits" from top business practitioners as well as my personal favorites. I want to share these final two lists with you. One is from Regina Anaejionu, affectionately known by her tribe as @ReginaTV and the second was from the ROAR

Christian Business Summit in Denver, CO in 2017. I added PR/Brand Strategist to the second list, because I believe that it is an important one that everyone needs to have at different phases within business, even if they are not on a monthly or quarterly retainer. If you have enjoyed reading about the aspects of the business and brand building but feel as if you still need help, that is okay. My team and I have put together some programs to help you along the way. If you are interested you can take a look at:
http://activatedream.com.

Now let's jump into those lists.

10 NECESSITIES FOR THE SELF-EMPLOYED BY REGINA ANAEJIONU

The items below are not all necessarily things you need on day one, but I do believe it's wise to put these all in place at some level.

1. Life Insurance
2. Business Insurance
3. Property Insurance
4. Health Insurance
5. Long-term Disability Coverage
6. Retirement
7. Accounting System
8. Separate Bank Account
9. Savings for Taxes
10. General Savings

SIX TYPES OF PEOPLE YOU NEED IN YOUR LIFE TO RUN YOUR BUSINESS SUCCESSFULLY

It may take you some time to secure all of these and that is okay. The main point is to let you know that they are needed, but you can still start without having all of these people ready to go in your life.

Your doctor: your health is everything. Nothing works if you don't work. It is imperative that you do all of your routine annual visits, this includes visiting the dentist twice a year for preventative care, and other specialists as needed.

Your lawyer: my dad taught me that an ounce of prevention is worth a pound of cure. Your attorney should be reviewing your contract, agreements, and leases; especially when you are getting started. A good attorney may cost you money on the front end, but I have I highly recommend you ask about retainers and special services for entrepreneurs.

Your accountant: this will be one of your best friends. They will advise you on the type of business entity you need, they will help you file the correct forms on your taxes, and they are single-handedly responsible for keeping you out of trouble with Uncle Sam.

Your therapist: is another preventative necessity. So many people ignore the stress that is caused by having a business, especially for those whose sole income is from self-employment.

It is critical to be a place of healing and growth when you are responsible for the business, employees, and projects. It is easy to become overwhelmed and sink in depression or paranoia. Your therapist can help you heal from past ones, and help you achieve optimal mental health in the present and future.

Your pastor/mentor: is essential for direction and vision. Like with all of these roles, this one should be chosen wisely. A good pastor/mentor can help you make process further faster, because they can tell you the pitfalls to avoid. They are also concerned about your total well-being, so they are able to instruct you in a holistic sense.

Your PR/Brand strategist: This is a person or agency that assists you with both the brand image and Public Relations parts of your business. Brand image is important to assist you with photoshoots, and components need for the publicity parts of your business.

Again, I hope this book has provided you with the tools you need to start do the work needed to create a tribe-based brand that will excel within a digital culture. I list every book, academic journal, and online article that I used to assemble this resource for you. For the last five years, I have committed to educating myself in these areas through conferences, workshops, webinars, trainings, and graduate studies in the field of Communication. While I am not an expert in all of these areas, I am an expert in creating a lasting business in a changing digital culture. My business model and tribe demographic has changed significantly over the last 15 years; however, my willingness to keep learning and serve by clients has not.

If you have taken notes, scribbled out a business or marketing plan, but feel as though you still need help; please do not fret. We are here to help. My team and I have created a number of resources to help you.

First, we offer coaching. I will walk you through a 4-week journey to getting your business started. Afterwards you have the option to extend your coaching or become enrolled in our Activate Your Brand academy that typically occurs three times a year (November, January, and March). Finally, you can receive information about our Activate Your Dream retreat that happens annually. The goal of the retreat is to help you escape from the cares of life and get your dream out of your head and heart and onto paper with actionable steps to bring it to fruition.

All of this information is available at http://activatedream.com, and if you would like to request a service that you do not see please email me directly at info@activatedream.com. Remember, I answer each email myself so please allow at least 1 business day for a reply. And if you don't need a service, you can still reach out to let me know the part of the book that was the most helpful to you. If email is not your thing you can also message me at @RainahMDavis on Facebook and Instagram. I would love to hear from you. Until next time, praying that you go out there, be great, and ACTIVATE!

REFERENCES FROM GRADUATE COURSEWORK

Online Media

Abell, M. (2017, March). You want to start a business—how should you finance it? *Entrepreneur.* Retrieved from: https://www.entrepreneur.com/article/290796

Beck, B. (2018, August). *Hootsuite vs. Buffer: We rated 10 key factors for each.* Clear Voice. Retrieved from: https://www.clearvoice.com/blog/hootsuite-vs-buffer-put-2-social-media-posting-tools-test/

Blumenthal, E. (2019, March). Facebook, Instagram were down most of Wednesday around the globe for many users. *USA Today.* Retrieved from: https://www.usatoday.com/story/tech/talkingtech/2019/03/13/facebook-instagram-go-down-across-united-states-apparent-outage/3151883002/

Davis, K. (2019). Fifty-two percent of women say that male co-workers with lower job titles earn more money. *Fast Company.* Retrieved from:

https://www.fastcompany.com/90326512/exclusive-fast-company-survey-52-of-women-have-found-out-that-a-man-below-them-makes-more-money

Detweiler, G. Co-working spaces: the office trend every entrepreneur needs to consider. *All Business.* Retrieved from: https://www.allbusiness.com/coworking-spaces-office-trend-every-entrepreneur-needs-to-consider-112108-1.html/2

Hill, S. (2018, August). Survey takes a look at the trends and challenges of black business ownership. *Black Enterprise.* Retrieved from:
https://www.blackenterprise.com/black-business-ownership-400-year/

Horton, A. (2019, April). "I had 15 years professional experience, but no one cared when I became a mom." *Fast Company.* Retrieved from:
https://www.fastcompany.com/90324442/former-goldman-sachs-employee-on-the-motherhood-penalty

Katz, K. (2018, March). Why Every Marketing Mix Should Include Paid, Owned & Earned Content. *Search Engine Journal.* Retrieved from:
https://www.searchenginejournal.com/paid-owned-earned-content/242075/

Lebowitz, S. (2018, August). There are 114 percent more women entrepreneurs than 20 years and it's not necessarily a good thing. *Inc.* Retrieved from:

https://www.inc.com/business-insider/more-women-entrepreneurs-today-than-20-years-ago-its-troubling.html

Pridham, D. (2018, January). Entrepreneurs: here's good news for 2018. *Forbes*. Retrieved from: https://www.forbes.com/sites/davidpridham/2018/01/10/entrepreneurs-heres-good-news-for-2018/#153d3fc86659

Zhou, M. & Wong, Q. (2019, March). Facebook blames server slipup for longest outage in its history. *CNET*. Retrieved from: https://www.cnet.com/news/cant-update-status-facebook-and-instagram-are-down/

Academic

Charmaine, d. P. (2017). The role of content marketing in social media content communities. *South African Journal of Information Management, 19*(1) Retrieved from: https://ezproxy.queens.edu:2048/login?url=https://search.proquest.com/docview/1950788529?accountid=38688

Charmaz, K. (4th Ed.). (2014). *Constructing Grounded Theory*. Thousand Oaks, California: Sage Publications.

Cody, S., & Goodwin, S. (2018). Taking a stand is taking a risk. *Risk Management, 65*(10), 4-6. Retrieved from:

https://ezproxy.queens.edu:2048/ login?url=https://search.proquest.com/ docview/2139007531?accountid=38688

Costin, G. (2012). The profile of an entrepreneur in a modern society. *Valahian Journal of Economic Studies, 3*(4), 13-16. Retrieved from: https://ezproxy.queens.edu:2048/ login?url=https://search.proquest.com/ docview/1399684587?accountid=38688

Escobar-Rodríguez, T., & Bonsón-Fernández, R. (2017). Facebook practices for business communication among fashion retailers. *Journal of Fashion Marketing and Management, 21*(1), 33-50. doi: http://dx.doi.org/10.1108/JFMM-11-2015-0087

Franklin, J. C., Mainelli, M., & Pay, R. (2014). Measuring the value of online communities. The Journal of Business Strategy, 35(1), 29-42. doi: http://dx.doi.org/10.1108/JBS-04-2013-0027

Ihlen, Ø., Fredriksson, M., & Ruler, B. V. (2009). Public relations and social theory: key figures and concepts. New York: Routledge.

Jahn, B., & Kunz, W. (2012). How to transform consumers into fans of your brand. *Journal of Service Management, 23*(3), 344-361. doi: http://dx.doi.org/10.1108/09564231211248444

Kilgour, M., Sasser, S. L., & Larke, R. (2015). The social media transformation process: Curating content into strategy. *Corporate Communications, 20*(3), 326-343. doi: http://dx.doi.org/10.1108/CCIJ-07-2014-0046

Ligon, G. S., Harms, M., & Derrick, D. C. (2015). Lethal brands: How VEOs build reputations. *Journal of Strategic Security, 8*(1-2), 27-42. doi: http://dx.doi.org/10.5038/1944-0472.8.1.1436

McArthur, J. A. (2014). Planning for strategic communication: a workbook for applying social theory to professional practice. Charlotte, NC: John A. McArthur.

Miller, V. (2011). *Understanding digital culture.* Los Angeles, CA: SAGE.

Muhammad, N. A., & Daniel, E. M. (2017). Ethnic entrepreneurs and online home-based businesses: An exploratory study. *Journal of Global Entrepreneurship Research, 7*(1), 1-21. doi: http://dx.doi.org/10.1186/s40497-017-0065-3

Myers, J. (2017). Brand yourself on YouTube: The design, execution, and reflection of a three- fold experiential exercise. *Journal of Marketing Development and Competitiveness, 11*(1), 11-18. Retrieved from: https://ezproxy.queens.edu:2048/login?url=https://search.proquest.com/docview/1930103855?accountid=38688

Paranjape, S. (2018). Role of digital marketing for developing customer loyalty. *Sansmaran Research Journal,* 1-7. Retrieved from:

https://ezproxy.queens.edu:2048/
login?url=https://search.proquest.com/
docview/2090328166?accountid=38688

Pfeffer, J., Zorbach, T., & Carley, K. M. (2014). Understanding online firestorms: Negative word-of-mouth dynamics in social media networks. *Journal of Marketing Communications*, 20(1-2), 117-128. http://dx.doi.org/10.1080/13527266.2013.797778 Retrieved from: https://ezproxy.queens.edu:2048/
login?url=https://search.proquest.com/
docview/1519507534?accountid=38688

Platon, O., PhD. (2015). An exploratory study regarding the brand-consumer relationship in social media. *Global Economic Observer,* 3(1), 135-140. Retrieved from: https://ezproxy.queens.edu:2048/
login?url=https://search.proquest.com/
docview/1690236428?accountid=38688

Plehn-dujowich, J. (2010). A theory of serial entrepreneurship. *Small Business Economics,* 35(4), 377-398. doi: http://dx.doi.org/10.1007/s11187-008-9171-5

Roundy, P. T. (2017). "Doing good" while serving customers. *Journal of Research in Marketing and Entrepreneurship,* 19(2), 105-124. Retrieved from: https://ezproxy.queens.edu:2048/
login?url=https://search.proquest.com/
docview/1973891211?accountid=38688

Rowley, J. (2004). Just another channel? marketing communications in e-business *Marketing Intelligence & Planning, 22*(1), 24-41. Retrieved from: https://ezproxy.queens.edu:2048/login?url=https://search.proquest.com/docview/213134589?accountid=38688

Scott, D. (1999). Do you need to be creative to start a successful business? *Management Research News, 22*(9), 26-41. Retrieved from: https://ezproxy.queens.edu:2048/login?url=?url=https://search.proquest.com/docview/223550312?accountid=38688

Watson, E., & Harris, J. (2009). The Oprah Phenomenon. Lexington, KY: The University Press of Kentucky.

Williams, C. C., & Nadin, S. (2011). Beyond the commercial versus social entrepreneurship divide. *Social Enterprise Journal, 7*(2), 118-129. doi: http://dx.doi.org/10.1108/17508611111156592

Wright, K. and Webb, L. (2011). *Computer-mediated communication in personal relationships.* New York: New York: Peter Lang Publishing, Inc.

Yan, J., & Yan, L. (2016). Individual entrepreneurship, collective entrepreneurship and innovation in small business: An empirical study. *International Entrepreneurship and Management Journal, 12*(4), 1053-1077. doi: http://dx.doi.org/10.1007/s11365-015-0380-5

Practitioners

Acuff, J. (2013). *Start: Punch fear in the face, escape average, do work that matters.* Brentwood, Tennessee, Lampo Press.

Airey, D. *Logo Design Love: A guide for creating iconic brand identities.* United States: New Riders.

Anaejionu, R. (2013). *The Small Business Manual and Workbook: How to plan, build, market your first business from scratch.* Austin, Texas: Hot Button Press.

Burg, B. (2006). *Endless Referrals: network your everyday contacts into sales.* New York, New York: McGraw-Hill.

Brunson, R. (2017). *Expert Secrets: The underground playbook to find your message, build a tribe, and change the world.* New York, New York: Morgan James Publishing.

Cardone, G. (2011). *The 10X Rule: The only difference between success and failure.* Hoboken, New Jersey: John Wiley & Sons, Inc.

Covey, S. (1992). *Principle-Centered Leadership.* New York, New York: Fireside—Simon & Schuster.

Deiss, R. (2015). *Invisible Selling Machine: five steps to crafting an automated, evergreen email campaign that literally makes sales while you sleep.* Austin, Texas: Digital Marketer Labs.

Ferris, T. (2009). *The 4-hour work week: Escape 9-5, live anywhere, and join the new rich.* New York, New York Harmony Books.

Godin, S. (2008). *Tribes: We need you to lead us.* Hudson, New York: Penguin Group.

Godin, S. (2012). *All Marketers tell stories: The underground classic that explains how marketing really works—and why authenticity is the best marketing of all.* New York, New York: Penguin Group.

Godin, S. (2012). *The Icarus deception: How high will you fly?* New York, New York: Penguin Group.

Godin, S. (2018). *This is Marketing: you can't be seen until you learn to see.* New York, New York: Penguin Group.

Hyatt, M. (2012). *Platform: Get Noticed in a noisy world—a step-by-step guide for anyone with something to say or sell.* Nashville, Tennessee: Thomas Nelson.

Iny, D. (2015). *The Audience revolution: The smarter way to build a business, make a difference, and change the world.* Montreal, Canada: Firepole Marketing.

Jantsch, J. (2010). The Referral Engine: *Teaching your business to market itself.* New York, New York: The Penguin Group.

Jiwa, B. (2014). *Difference: The one page method for reimaging your business and reinventing your marketing.* Columbia, South Carolina: The Story of the Telling Press.

Jones, S. (2012). *Brand like a rock star: Lessons from rock 'n' roll to make your business rich and famous.* Austin, Texas: Greenleaf Book Group Press.

Kelley, T. and Kelley, D. (2013). *Creative Confidence: Unleashing the creative potential within us all.* New York: Crown Business.

Kerpen, D. (2011). *Likeable social media: How to delight your customers, create an irresistible brand, and be generally amazing on Facebook (and other social networks).* United States McGraw-Hill.

Kleon, A. (2012). *Steal like an artist: 10 things nobody told you about being creative.* New York, New York: Workman, Publishing Co.

Larter, L. (2016). *Pilot to profit: Navigating modern entrepreneurship to build your business using online marketing, social media, content marketing and sales.* New York, New York: Morgan James Publishing.

Lederman, G. (2007). *Achieve Brand Integrity: Ten truths you must know to enhance employee Performance and increase company profits.* Rochester, New York: B@W Press.

Martin, G. (2010). *30 days to social media success: The 30 day results guide to making the most of Twitter, Blogging, LinkedIn, and Facebook.* Pompton Plains, New Jersey: The Career Press Inc.

Michalowicz, M. (2012). *The Pumpkin plan: A simple strategy to grow a remarkable business in any field.* New York, New York: The Penguin Group.

Neumeier, M. (2003). *The Brand gap: How to bridge the distance between business strategy and design.* Indianapolis, Indiana: New Riders Publishing.

Port, M. (2011). *Book Yourself Solid: The fastest, easiest, and most reliable system for getting Clients than you can handle even if you hate marketing and selling.* Hoboken, New Jersey: John Wiley & Sons.

Reed, T. V. (2014). *Digitized lives: Culture, power and social change in the internet era.* New York: Routledge.

Ries, A. and Riles, L. (2002). *The 22 Immutable Laws of branding: How to build a product or service into a world-class brand.* New York: New York: HarperCollins Publishers Inc.

Safko, L. (2012). *The Social media Bible: Tactics, tools & strategies for business success.* Hoboken, New Jersey: John Wiley & Sons.

Signorelli, J. (2014). *Story branding 2.0: Creating stand-out brands through the power of the story.* Evanston, Illinois: Story-Lab Publications.

Simmons, A. (2015). *Whoever tells the best story wins: How to use your own stories to communicate with power and impact.* Broadway, New York: American Management Association.

Solis, B. (2013). *What's the Future of Business? Changing the Way Businesses Create Experiences.* Hoboken, NJ: John Wiley & Sons, Inc.

Walter, E. and Gioglio. *The Power of Visual Storytelling: How to use visuals, videos, and Social Media to market your brand.* McGraw-Hill Education.

Vaynerchuk, G. (2009). *Crush It: Why now is the time to cash in on your passion.* New York, New York: Harper Collins.

Yohn, D.L. (2014). *What Great Brands Do: The Seven Brand-Building Principles that Separate the Best from the Rest.* San Francisco, CA: Jossey-Bass.

ADDITIONAL REFERENCES (POST GRADUATE WORK)

Online Articles

https://www.vox.com/the-goods/2019/8/28/20836936/popeyes-chick-fil-a-fried-chicken-sandwich-twitter

https://www.forbes.com/sites/forbesagencycouncil/2017/02/23/the-art-of-rebranding-how-to-be-smart-and-strategic/#2d6079635eee

https://www.cnn.com/2019/08/27/business/popeyes-chicken-sandwich-sold-out-trnd/index.html

https://www.livemint.com/technology/tech-news/tiktok-s-15-second-videos-a-rage-but-govt-isn-t-amused-1566926584018.html

https://www.businessnewsdaily.com/1523-method-cleaning-products-founders.html

http://www.slate.com/articles/technology/top_right/2011/07/eric_ryan_cofounder_of_method.html

https://www.daveramsey.com/blog/what-is-passive-income

https://sproutsocial.com/insights/instagram-stats/

https://sproutsocial.com/insights/facebook-stats-for-marketers/

https://blog.hootsuite.com/linkedin-statistics-business/

https://www.brandwatch.com/blog/youtube-stats/

www.ingramcontent.com/pod-product-compliance
Lightning Source LLC
Chambersburg PA
CBHW050438010526
44118CB00013B/1585